EMPTY FRAMES

Edited by John Clayman

Empty Frames.

Printed in an edition of 1000 by Calverts, London E2.

A catalogue record of this book is available at the British Library.

Published by MOT International

Unit 54/5th Floor Regents Studios
8 Andrews Road
London E8 4QN

ISBN 0-9554061-0-2 978-0-9554061-0-2

Ashiya, Japan. 1955

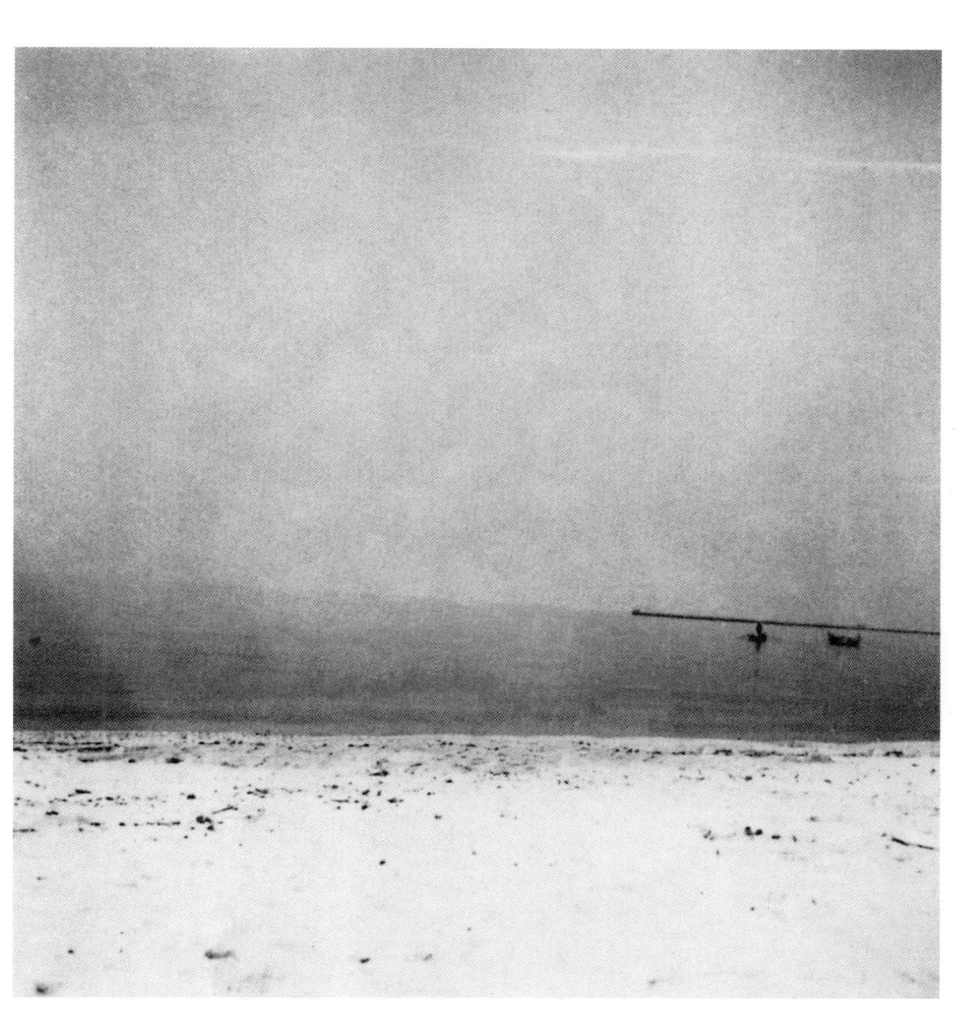

Paris, France. January 26th 1962

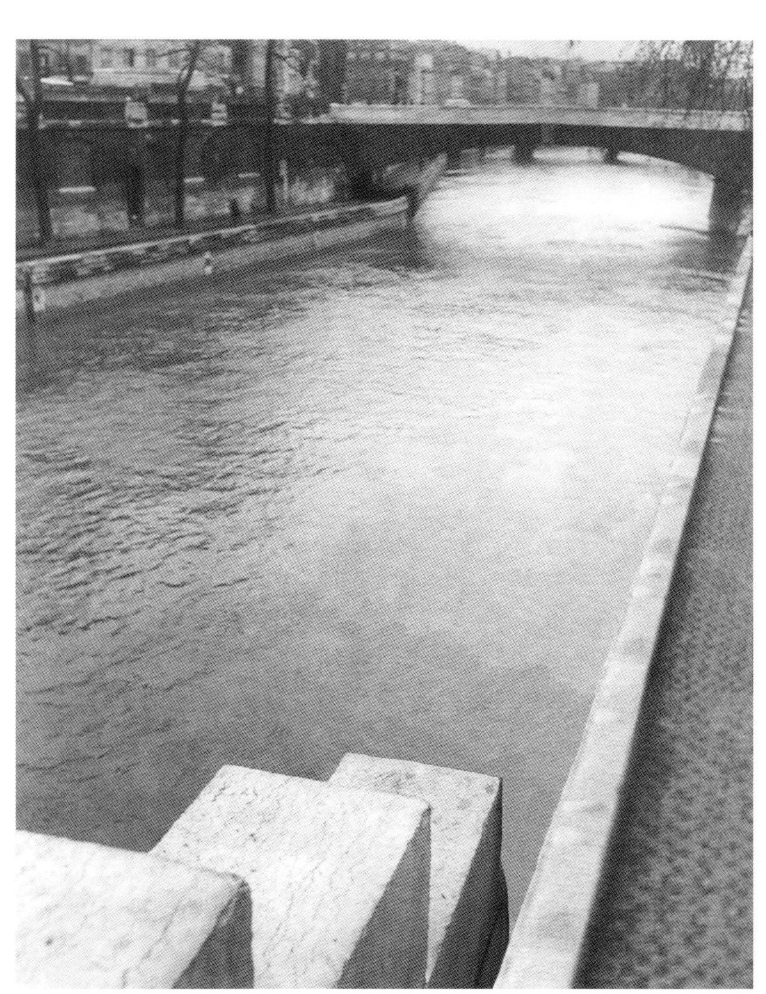

England. 1967

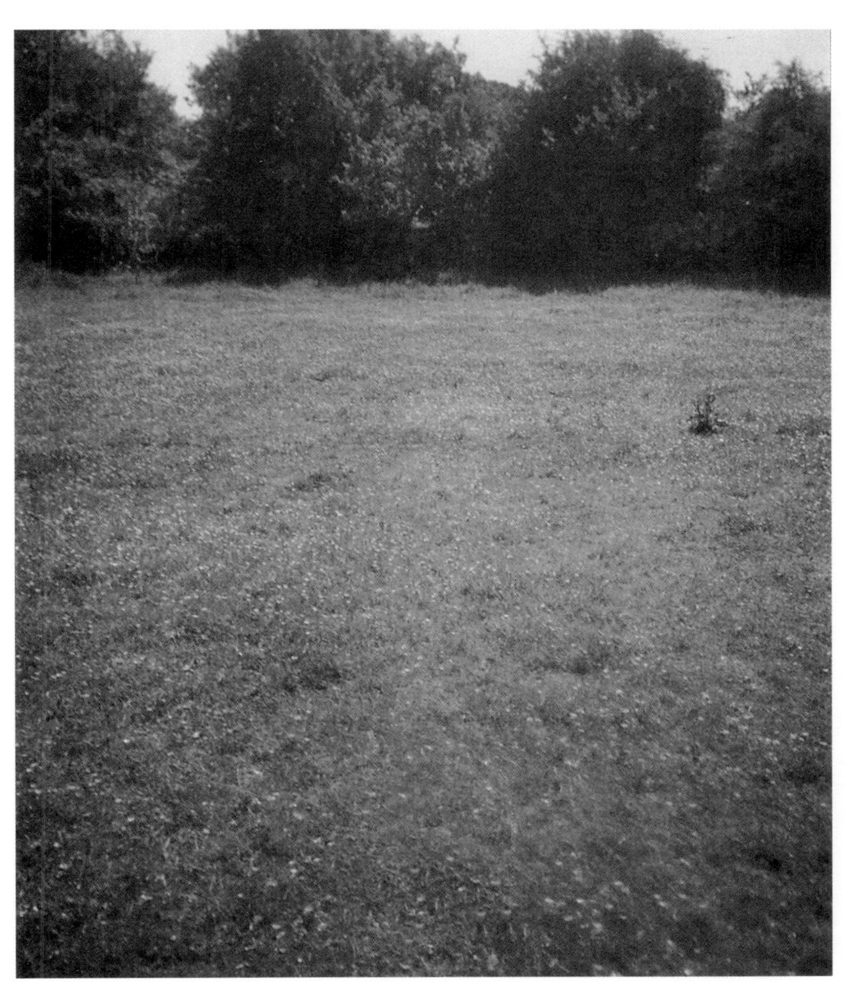

Sierra Mountains, near Reno, Nevada, USA. 1967

Mojave Desert, California, USA. 1968

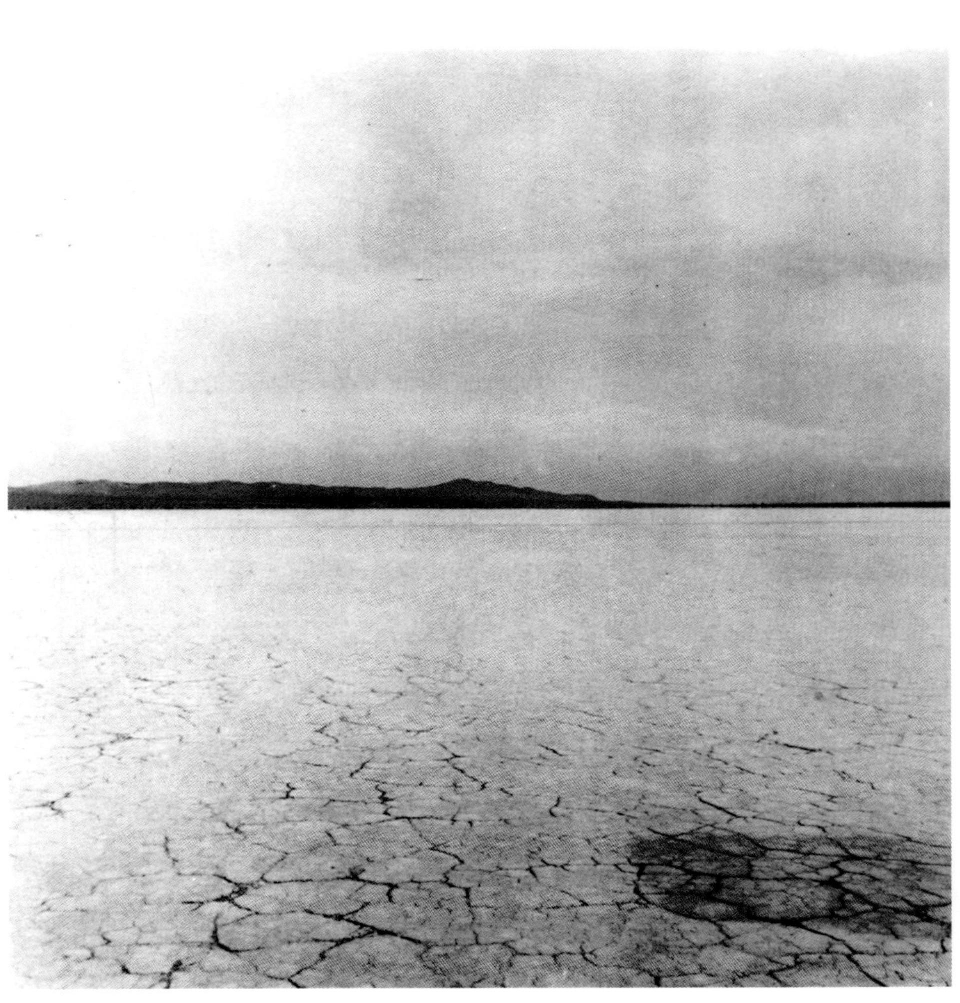

England. 1968

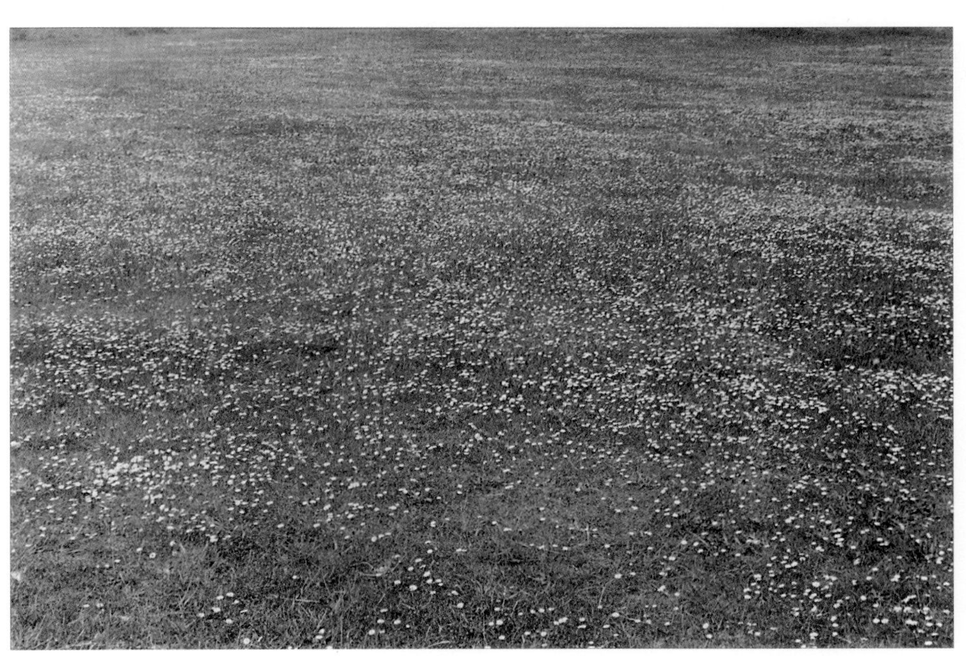

Black Rock Desert, Nevada, USA. 1968

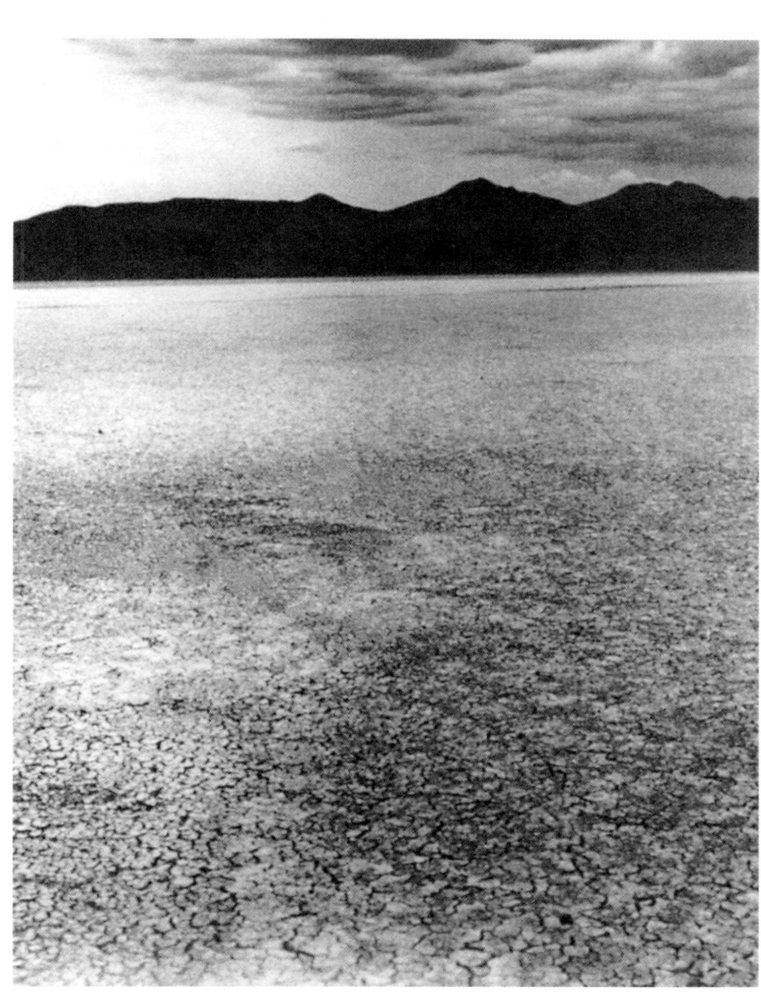

Vancouver, Canada. 1969

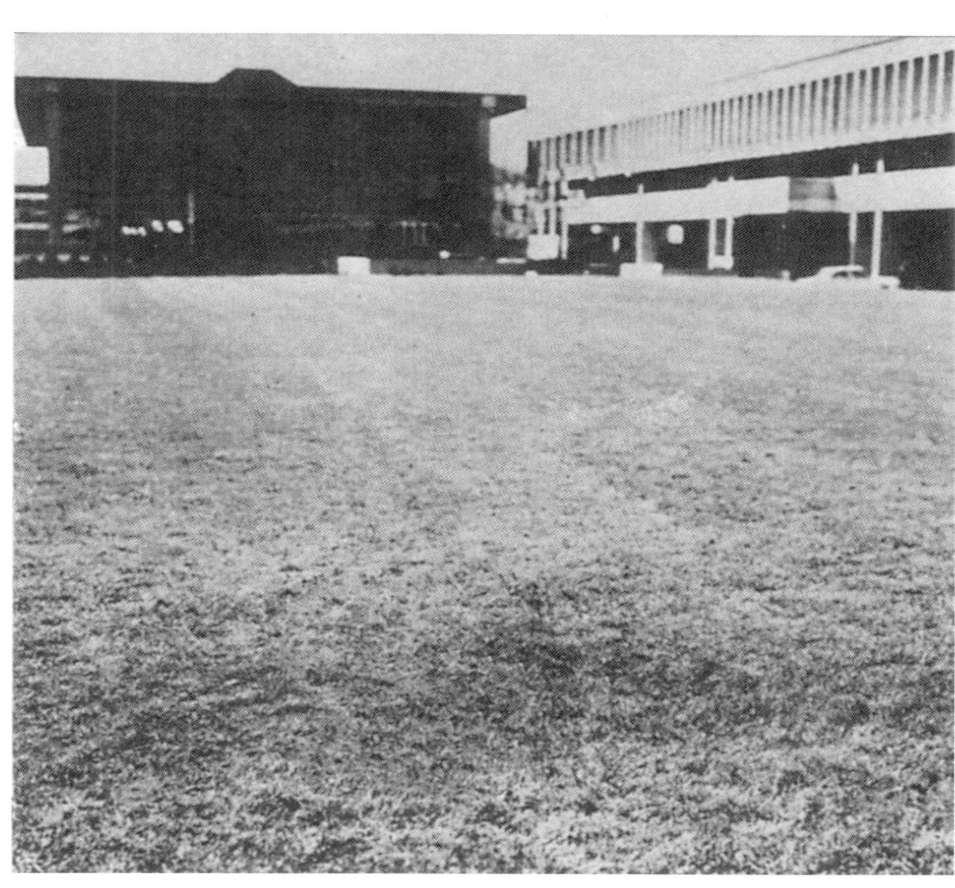

Cayuga Rock Salt Mine, Ithaca, NY, USA. February 1969

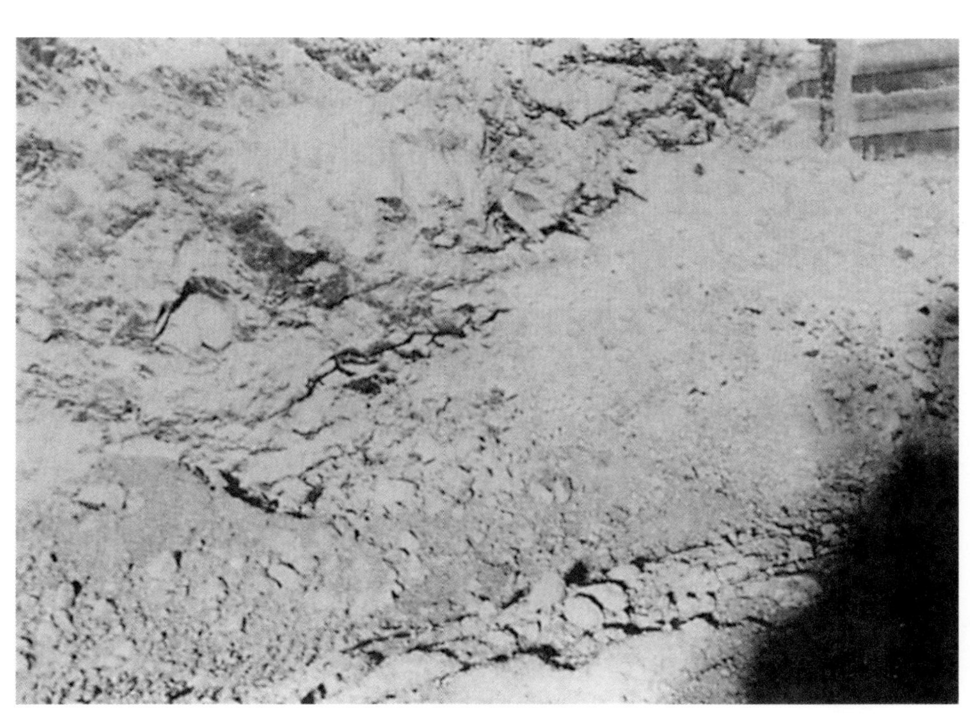

Finsterwolde, Holland. 1969

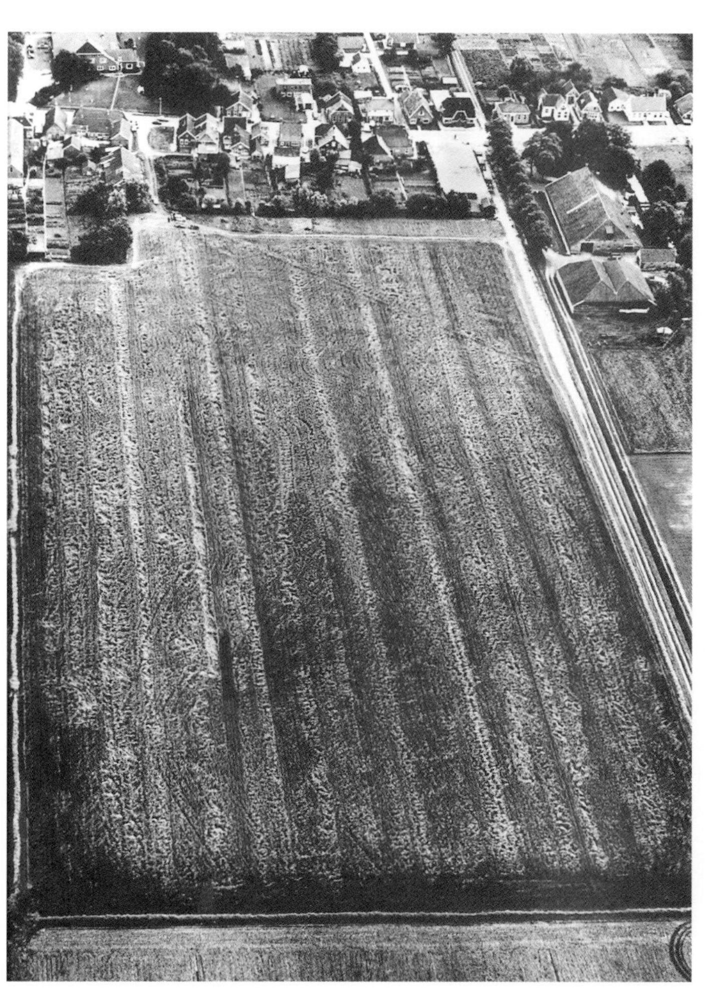

Germany. 1970

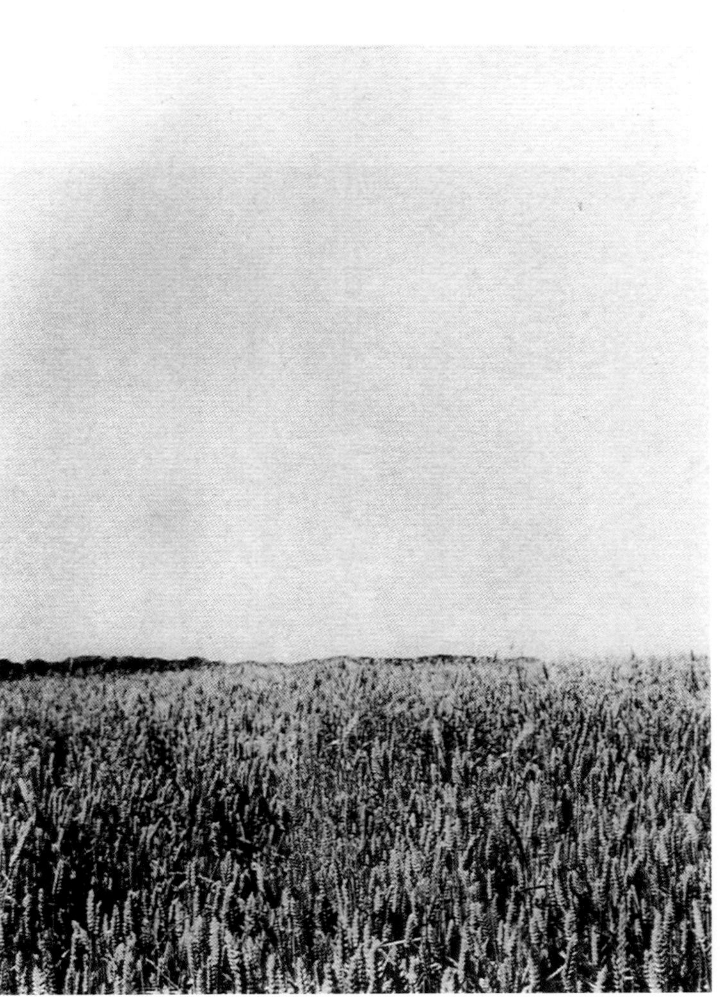

Opera, Paris, France. 1970

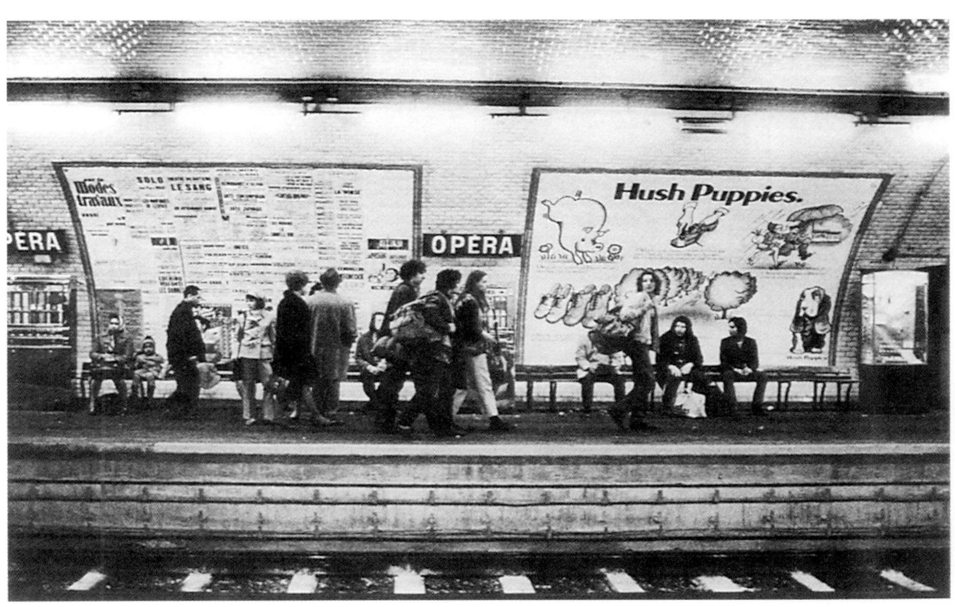
PERA
Modes travaux
SOLO
LE SANG
OPERA
Hush Puppies.

Long Island, New York, USA. 1970

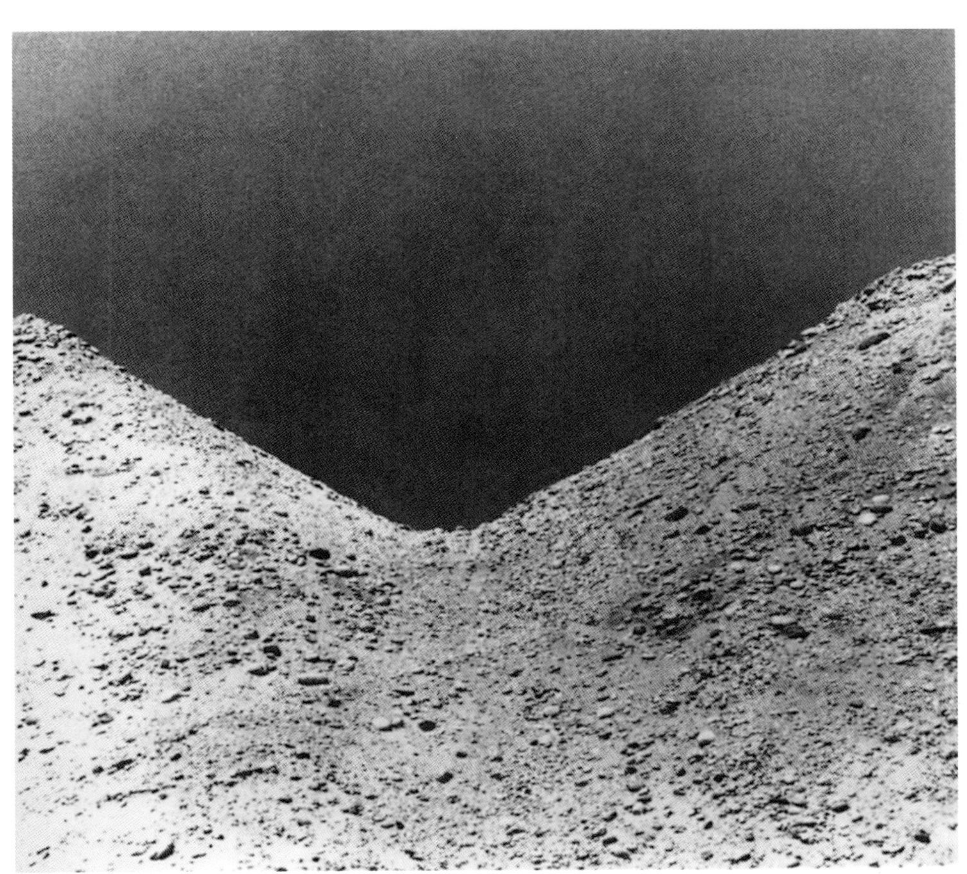

Ramona, California, USA. 1970

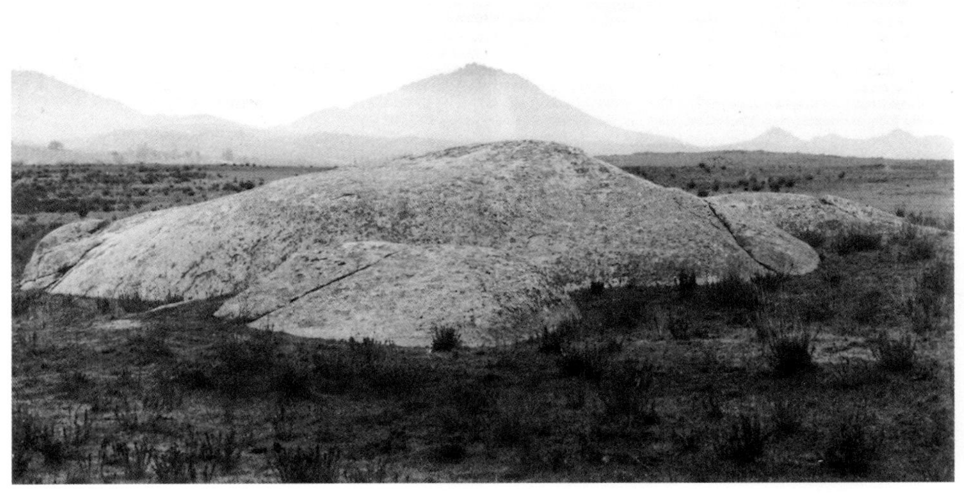

Via de la Valle, California, USA. May 17th 1971

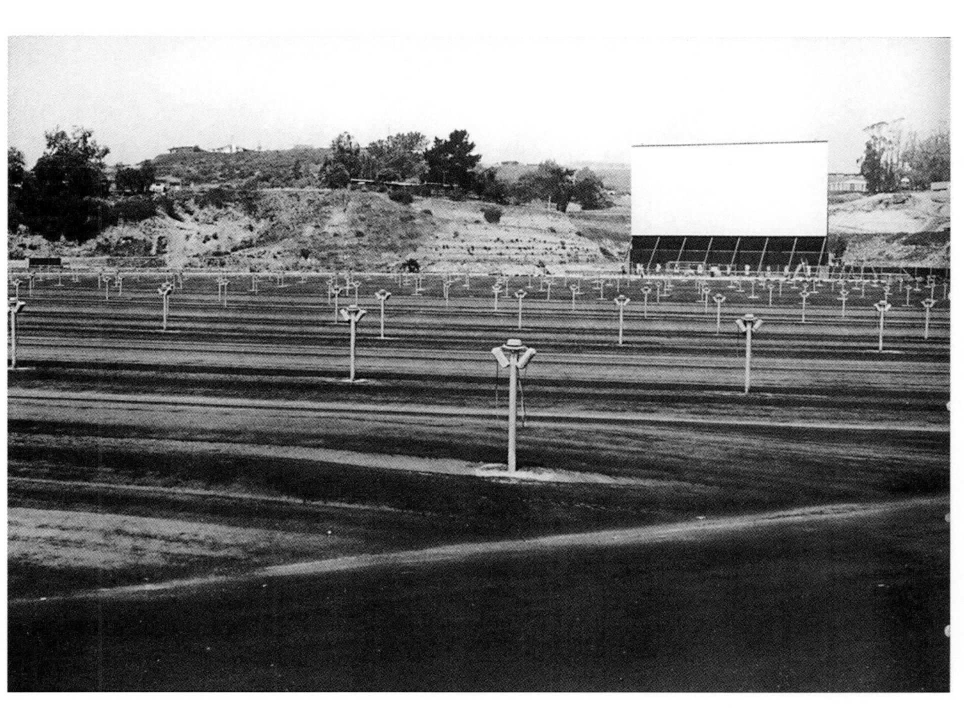

Amsterdamse Bos, Holland. 1971

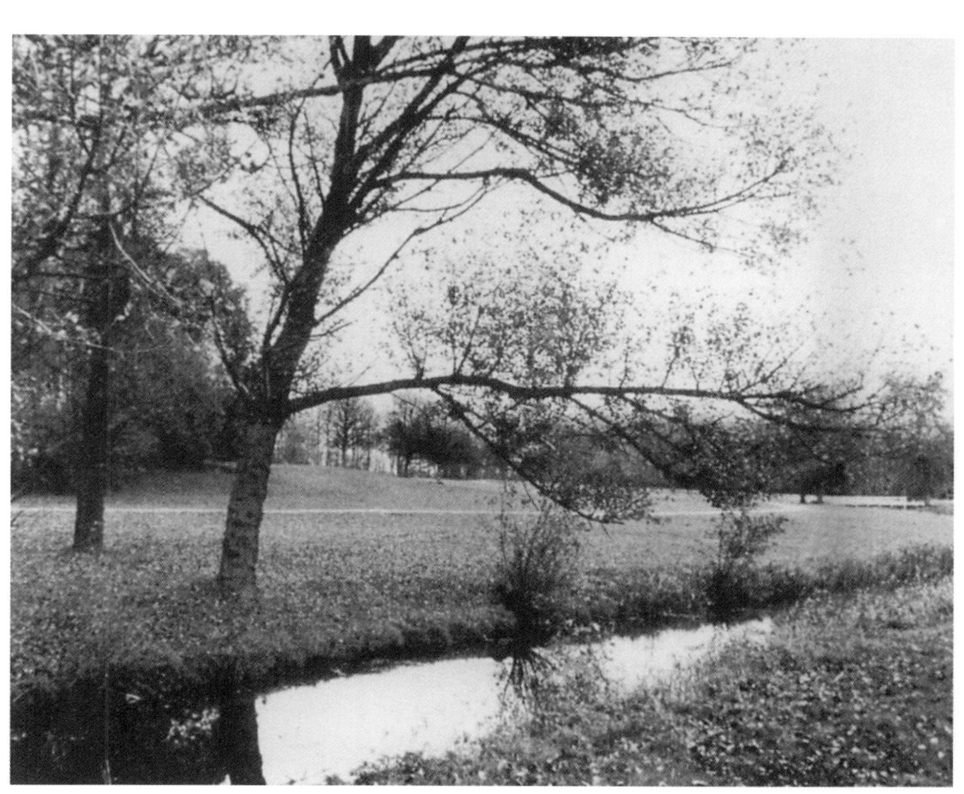

La Jolla, California, USA. July 6th 1972

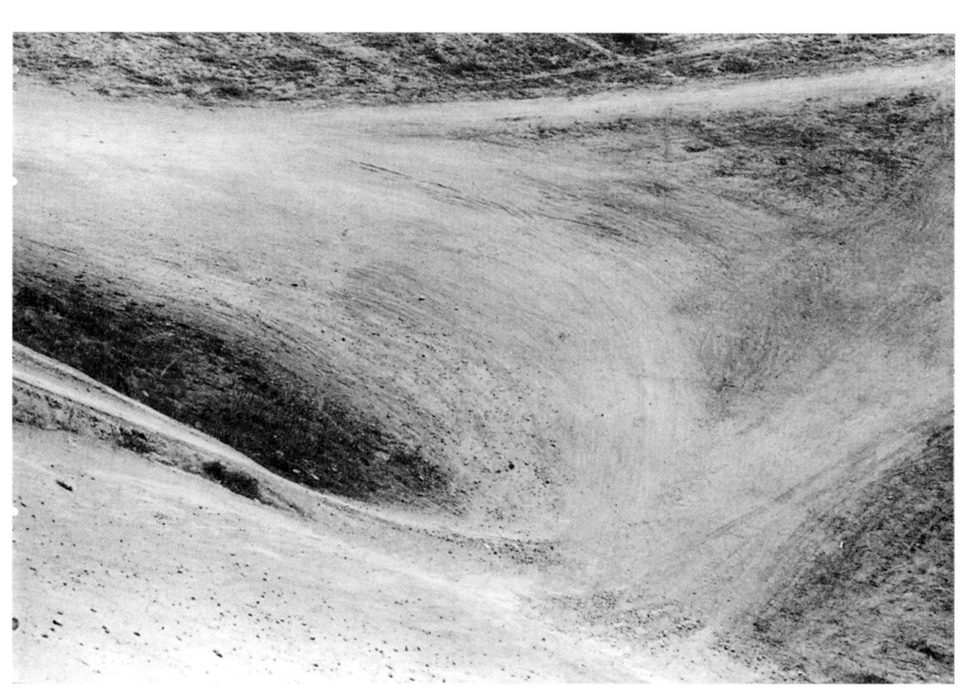

Bolivia. 1972

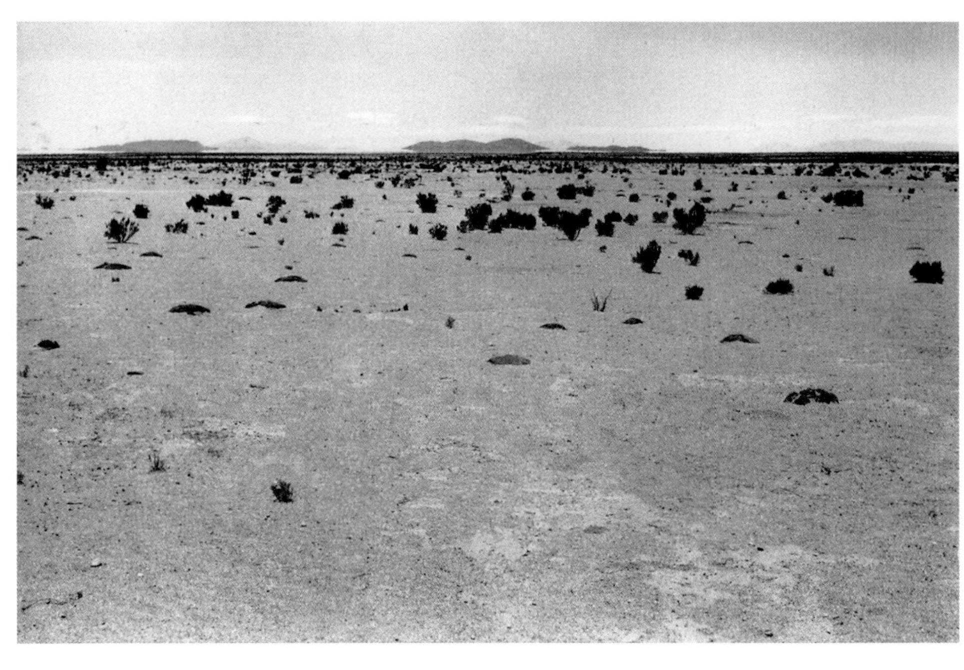

Los Angeles, California, USA. January 5th 1973

Roslyn, New York, USA. 1977

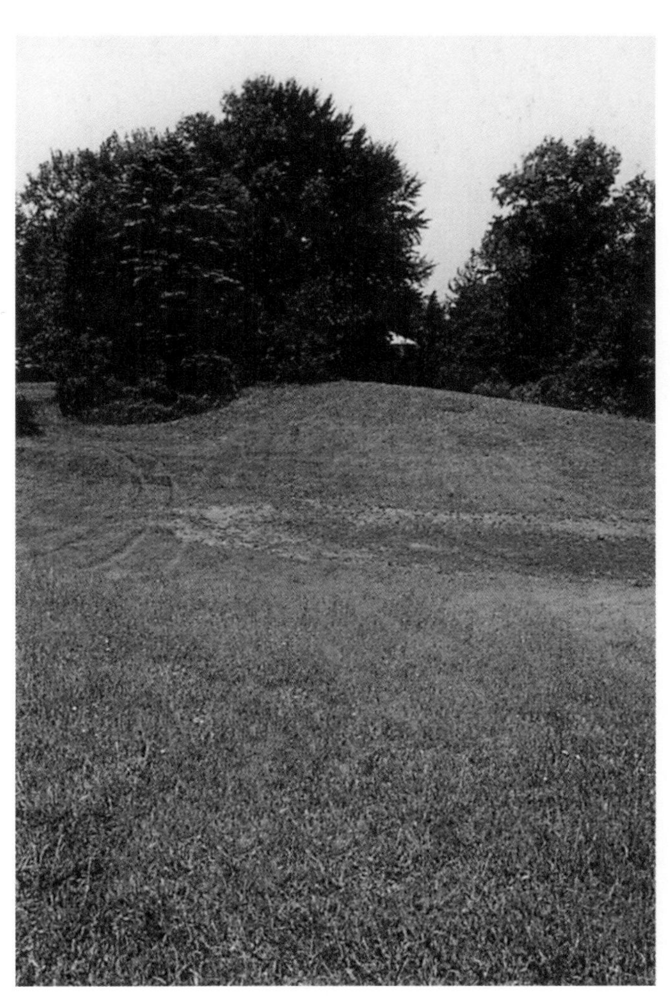

El Mirage Dry Lake, California, USA. 1978

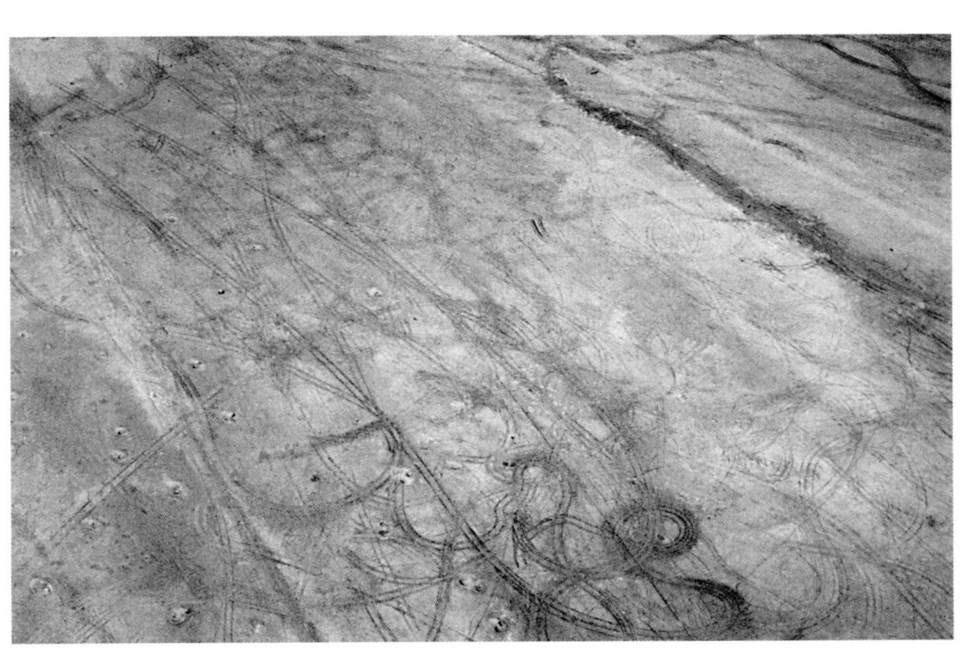

Washington Square Plaza, NYC, USA. 1981

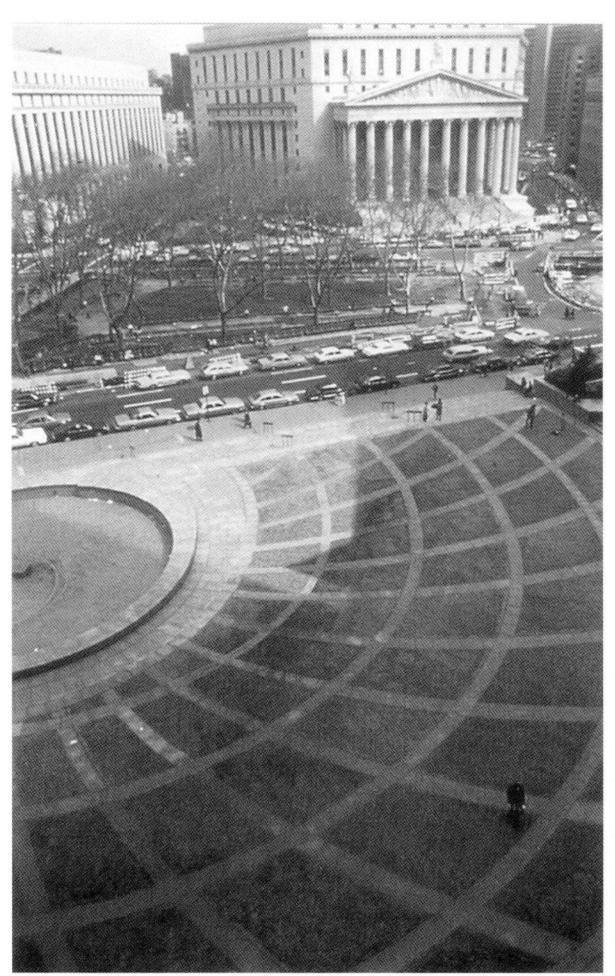

Nuclear Test Site, Nevada, USA. February 14th 1996

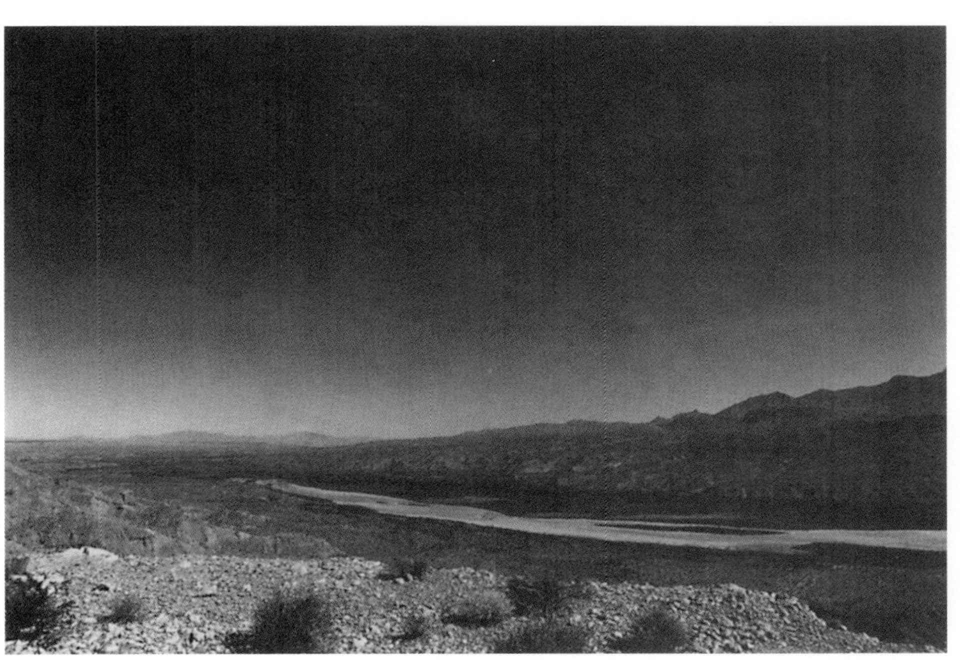

New York, USA. April 20th 1996

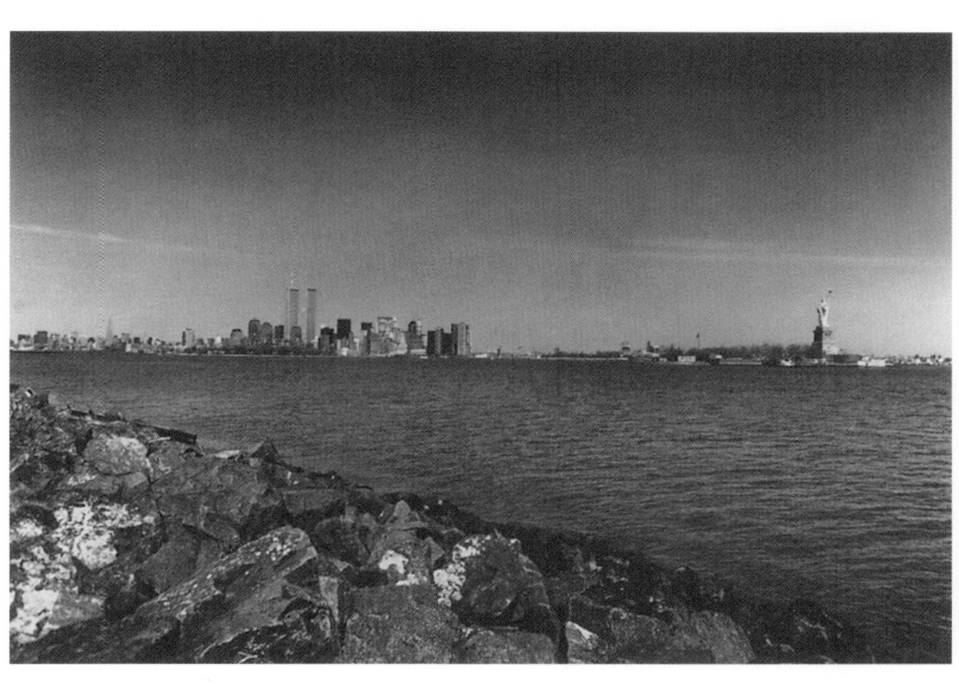

London, England. 1993

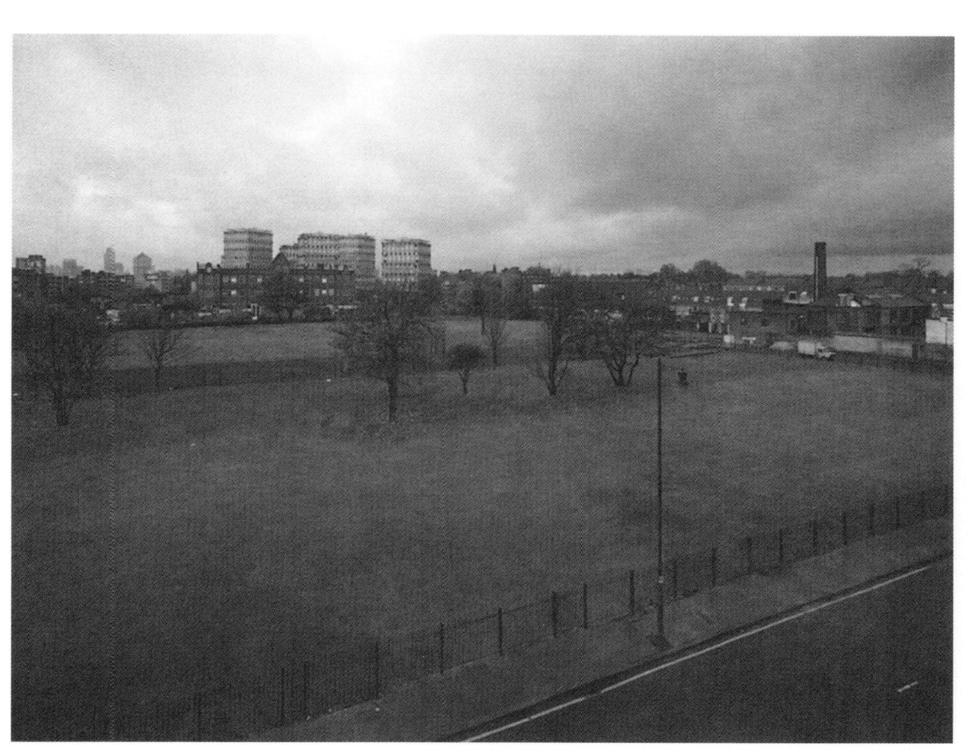

New York, USA. 1979

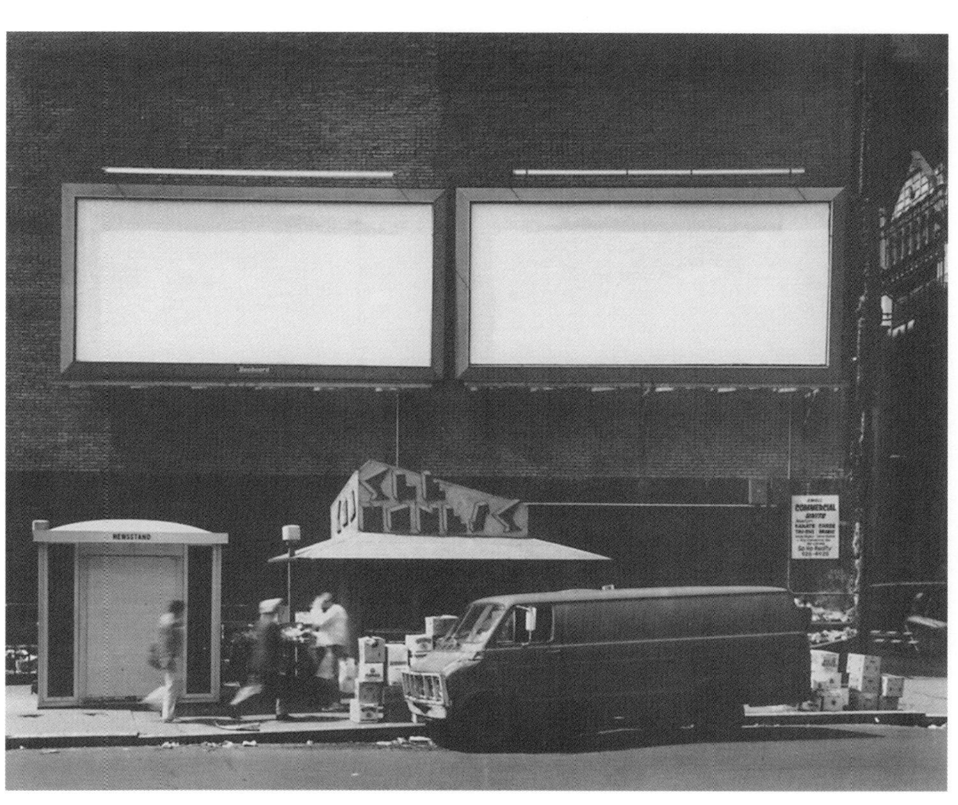
NEWSSTAND
COMMERCIAL

Nassau County Museum, Roslyn, New York, USA. 1978

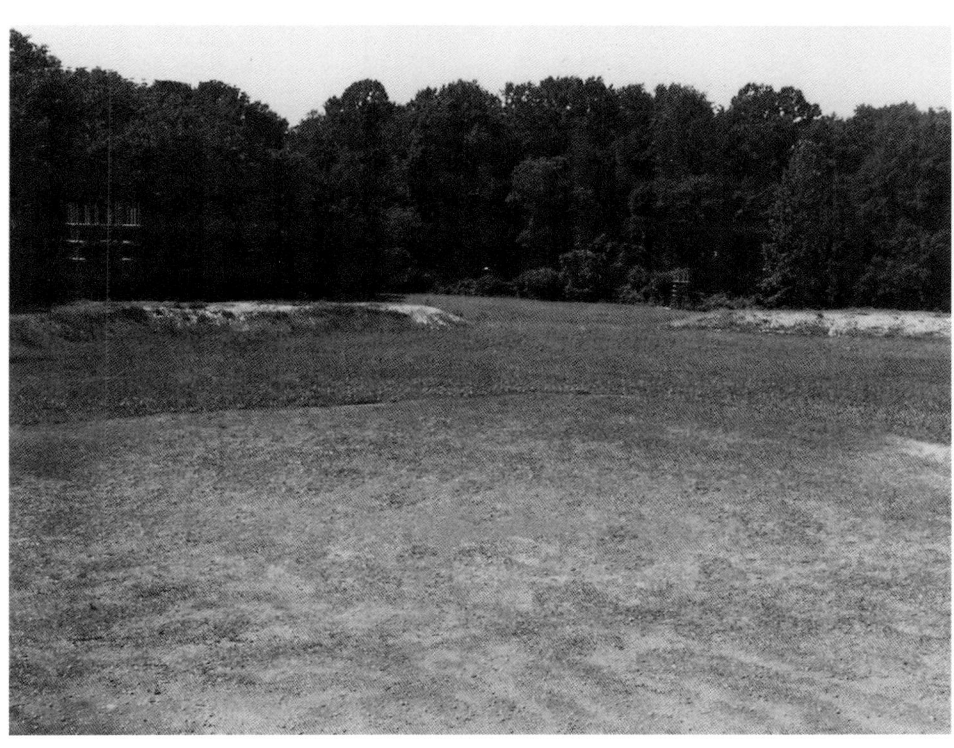

Near Quemado, New Mexico, USA. 1977

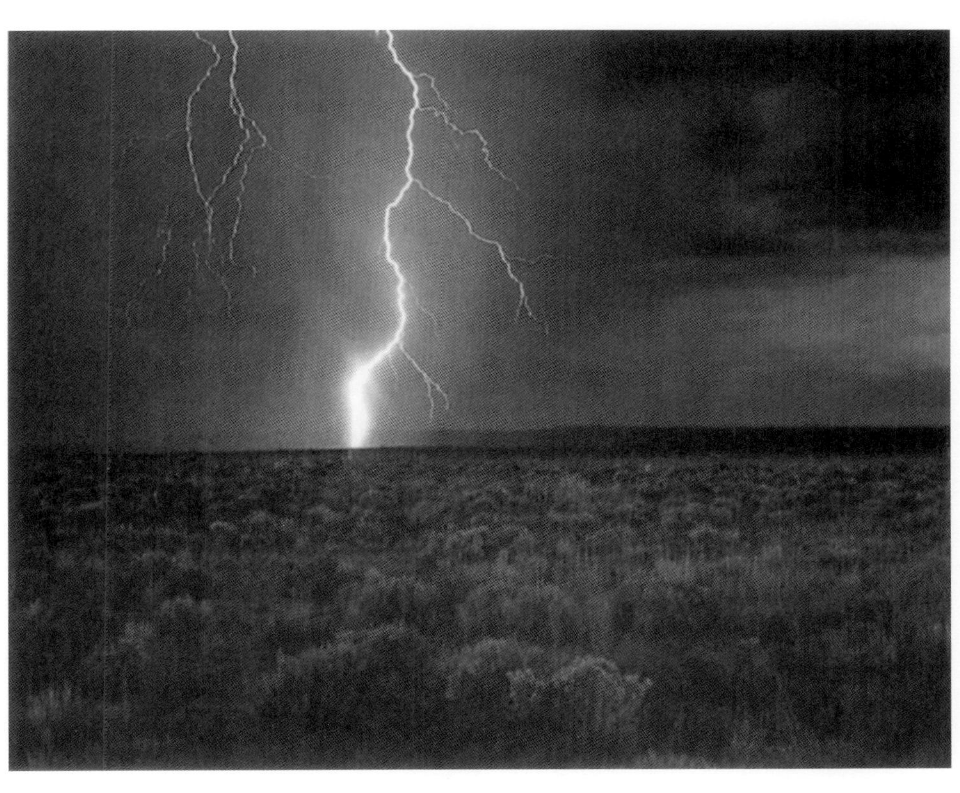

Humphrey Street, Englewood, New Jersey, USA. 1974

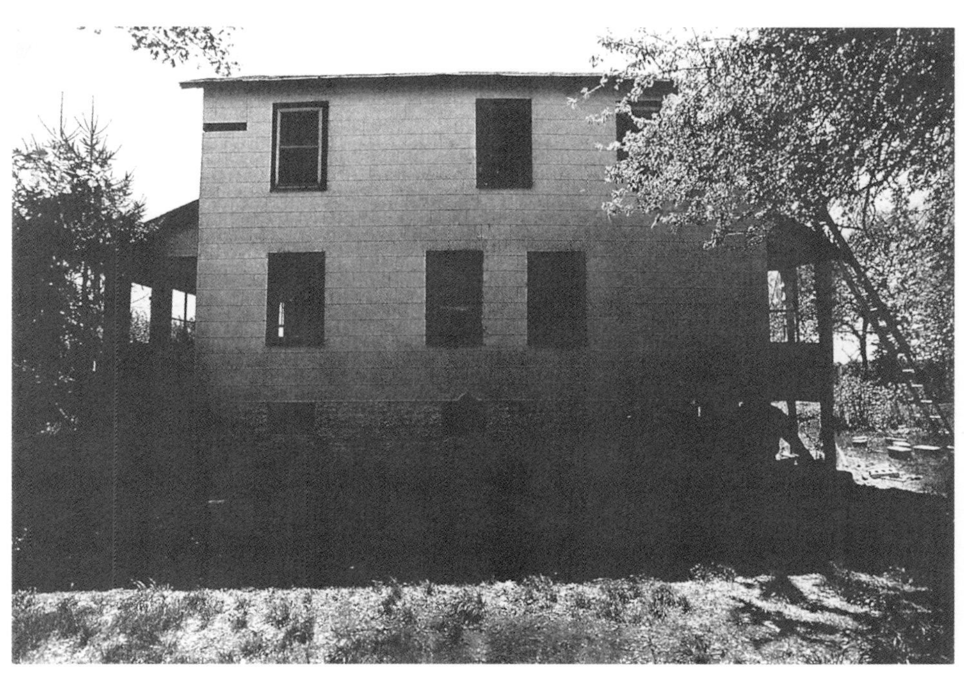

Amarillo, Texas, USA. 1973

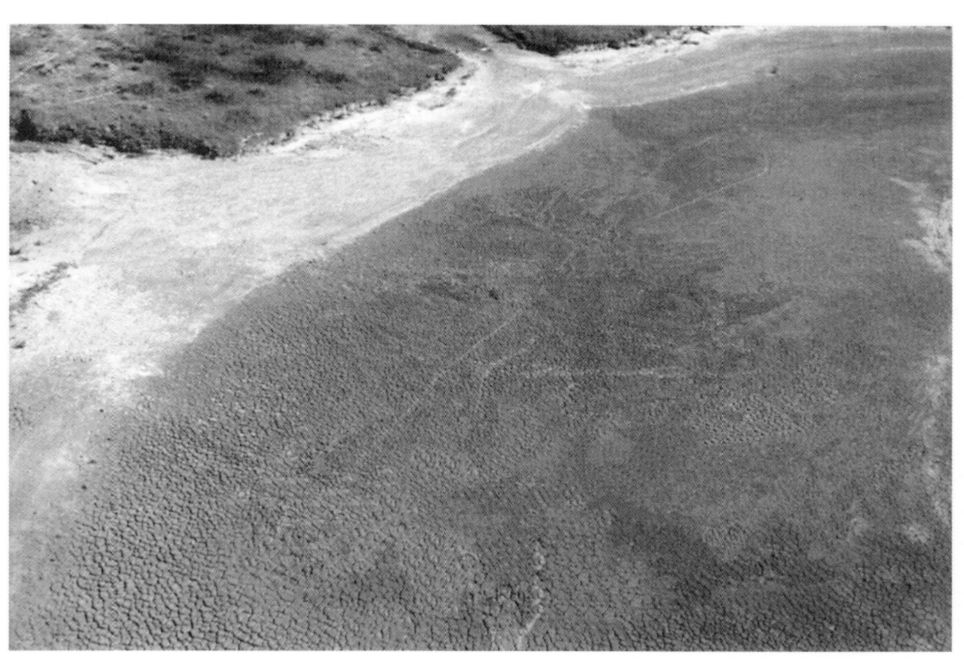

Gibney Farm, near New Kingston, Pennsylvania, USA. 1972

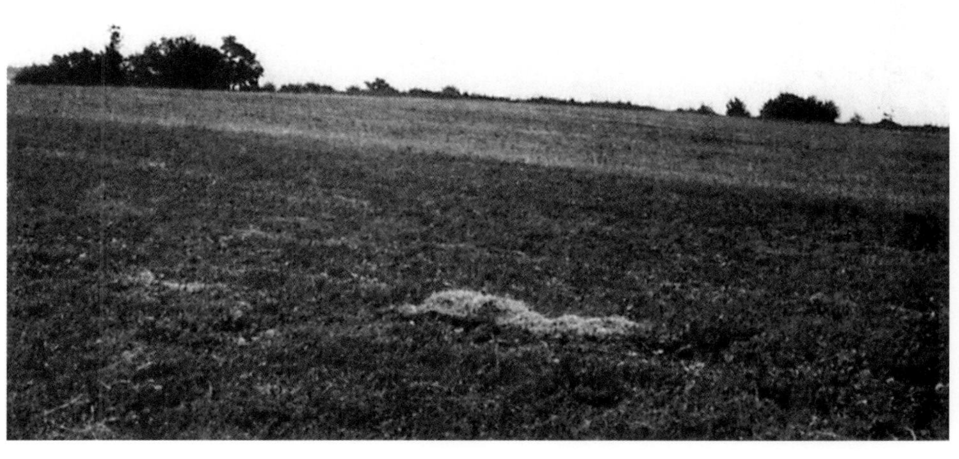

Peru. 1972

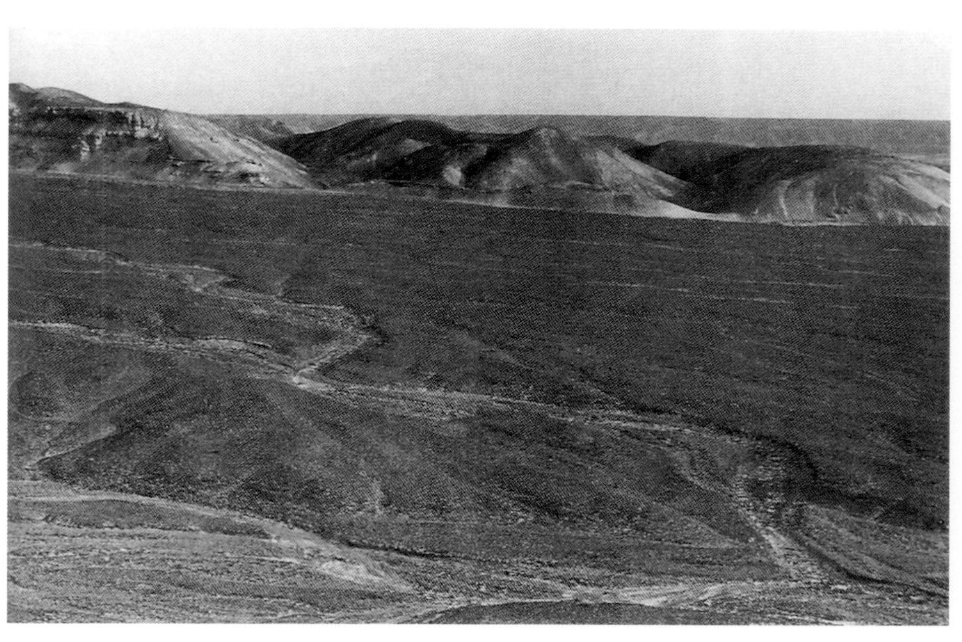

Signal Hill, California, USA. February 15th 1972

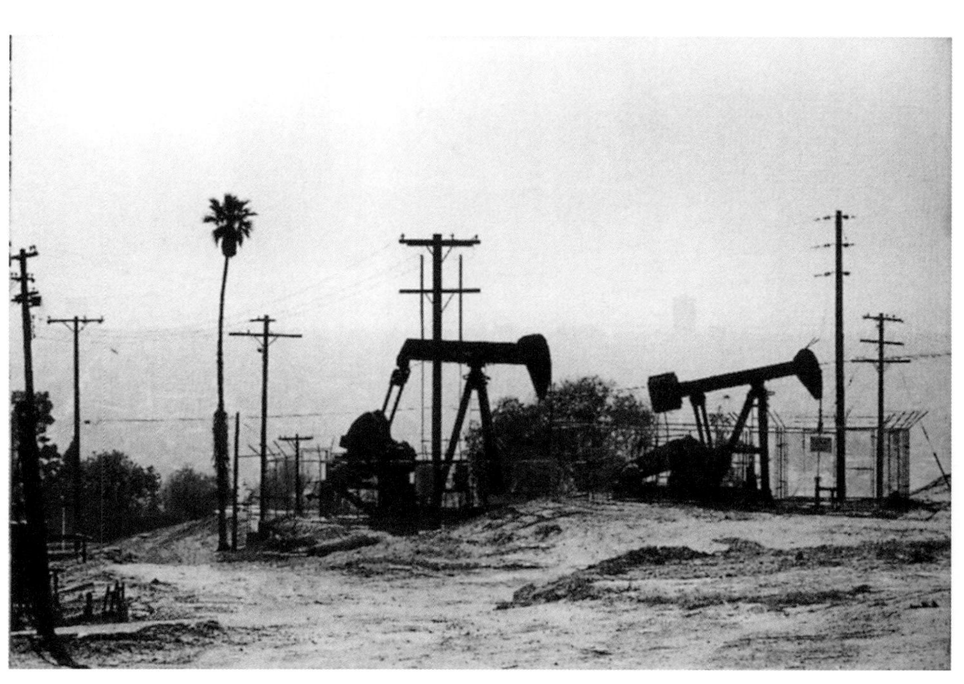

Ireland. 1971

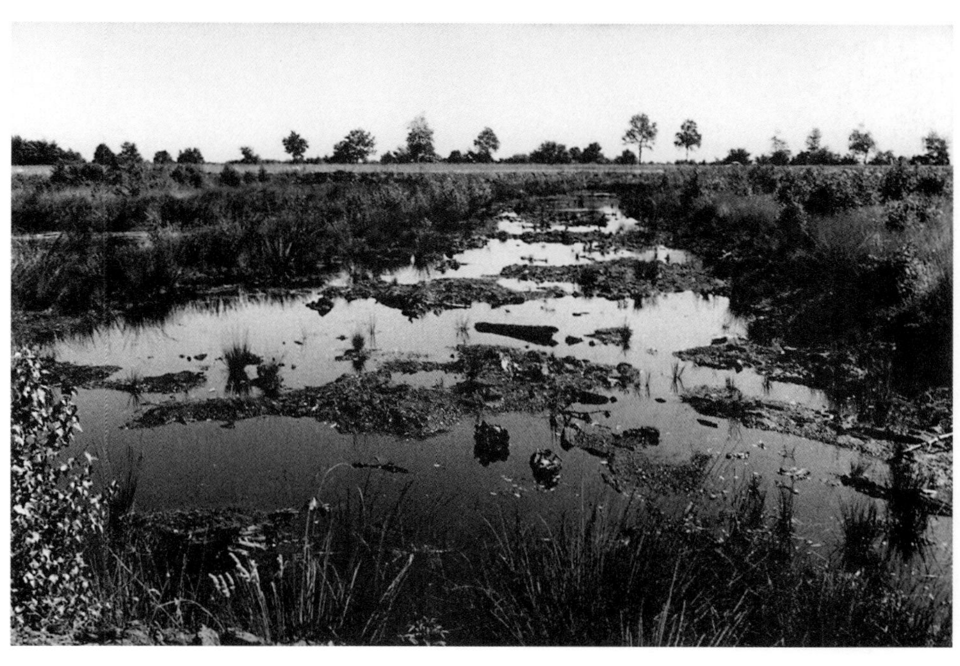

Amsterdam, Holland. 1970

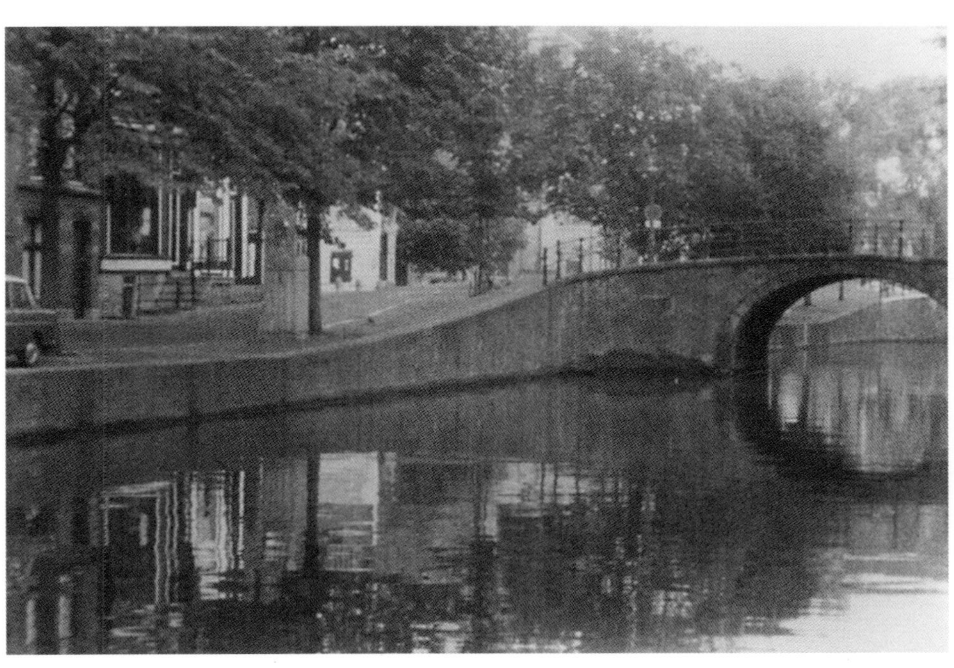

Whitewater, Wisconsin, USA. 1970

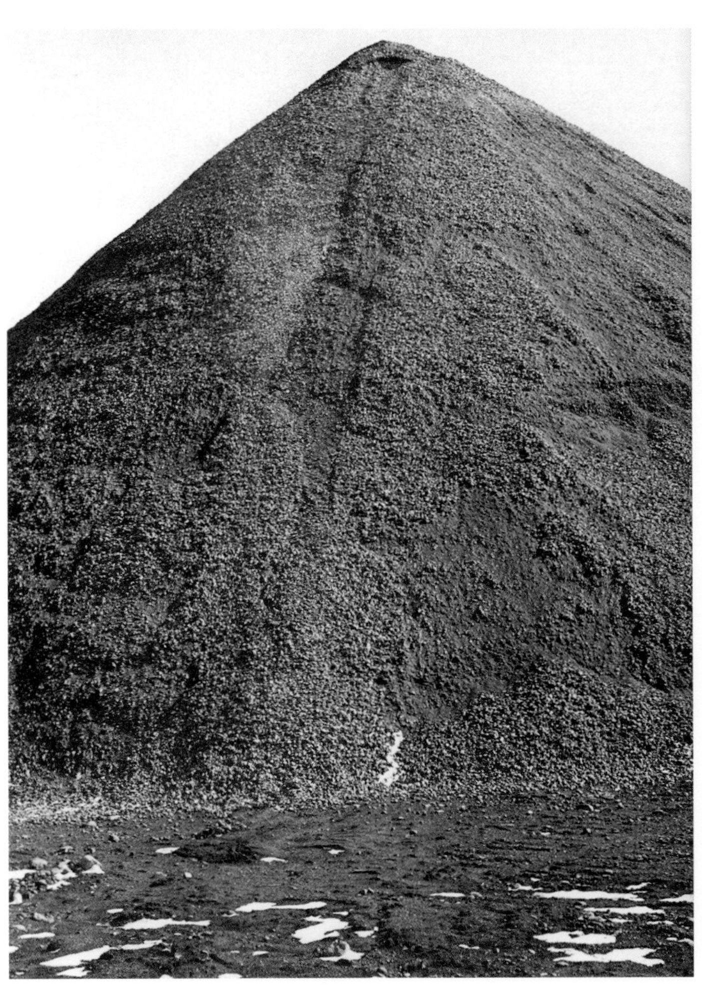

Great Salt Lake, Utah, USA. 1970

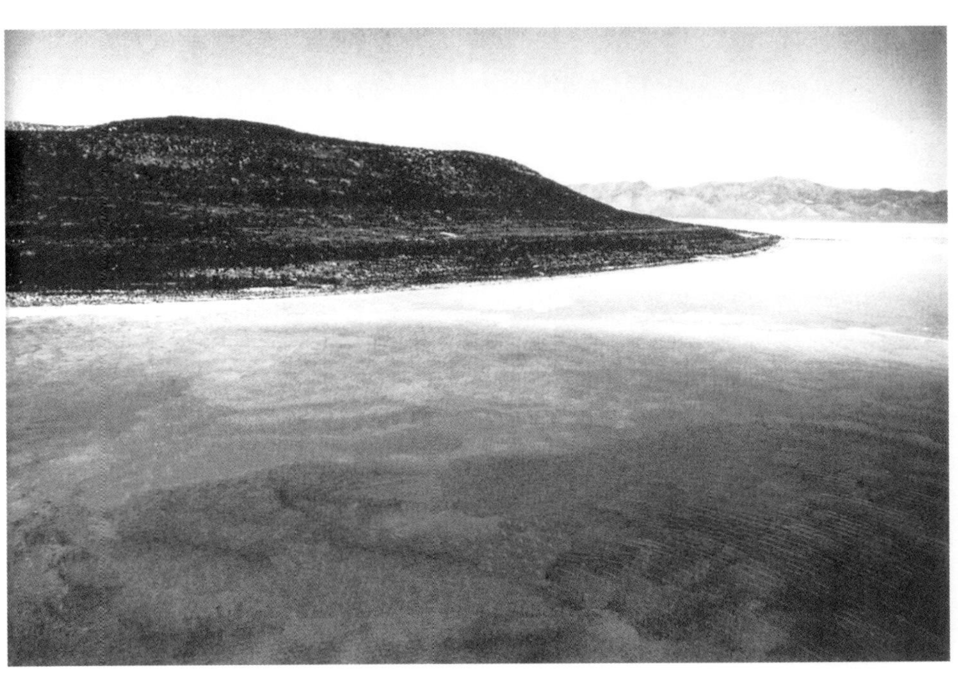

San Pablo, California, USA. 1969

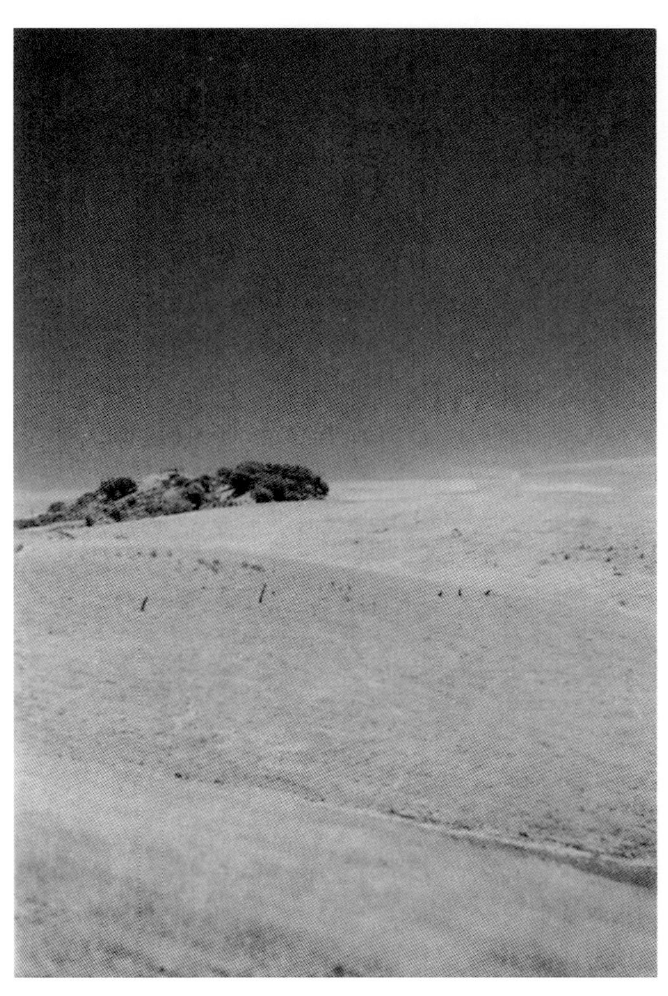

Berne, Switzerland. 1969

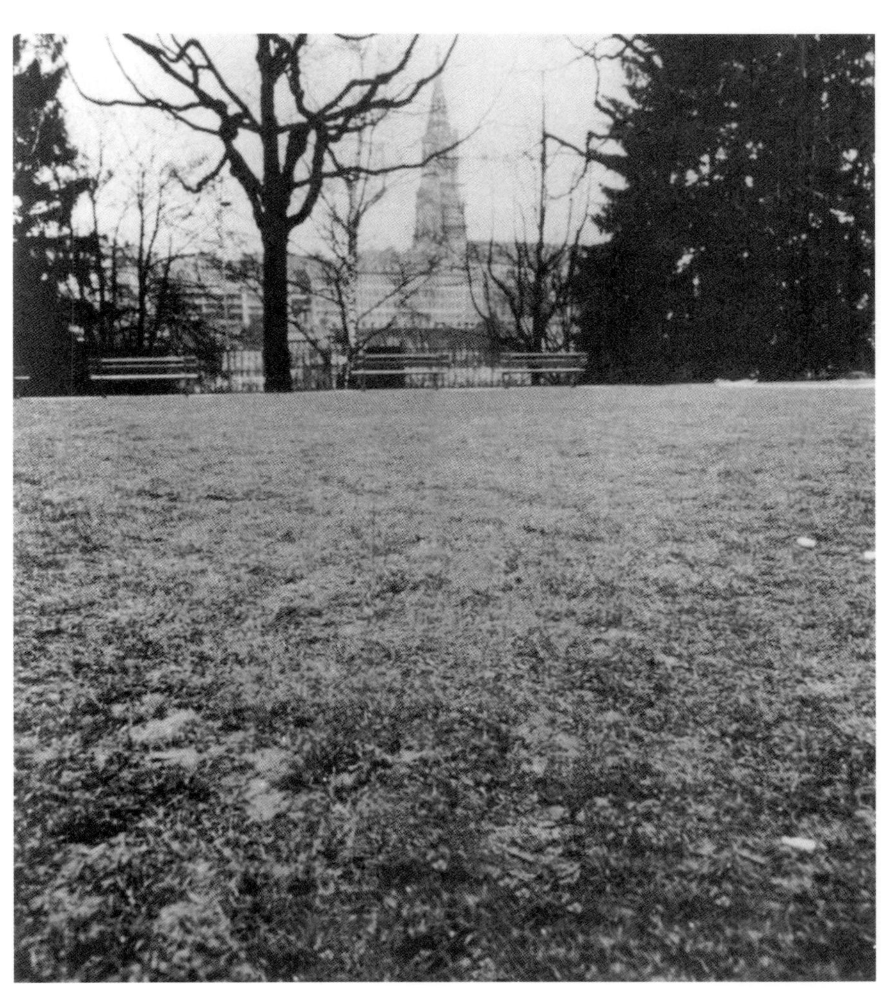

Rome, Italy. 1969

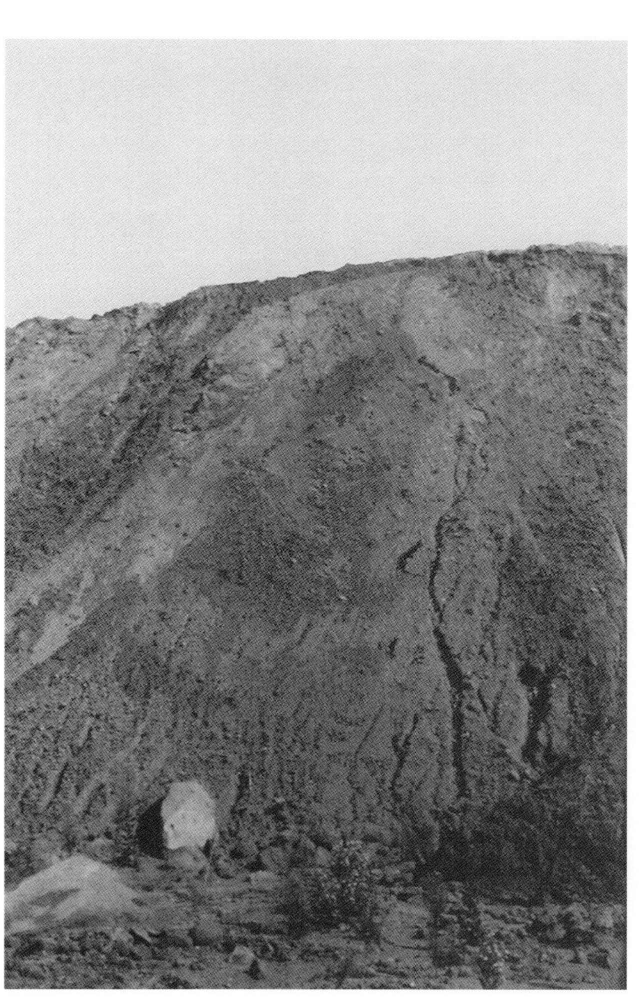

Aspen, Colorado, USA. 1968

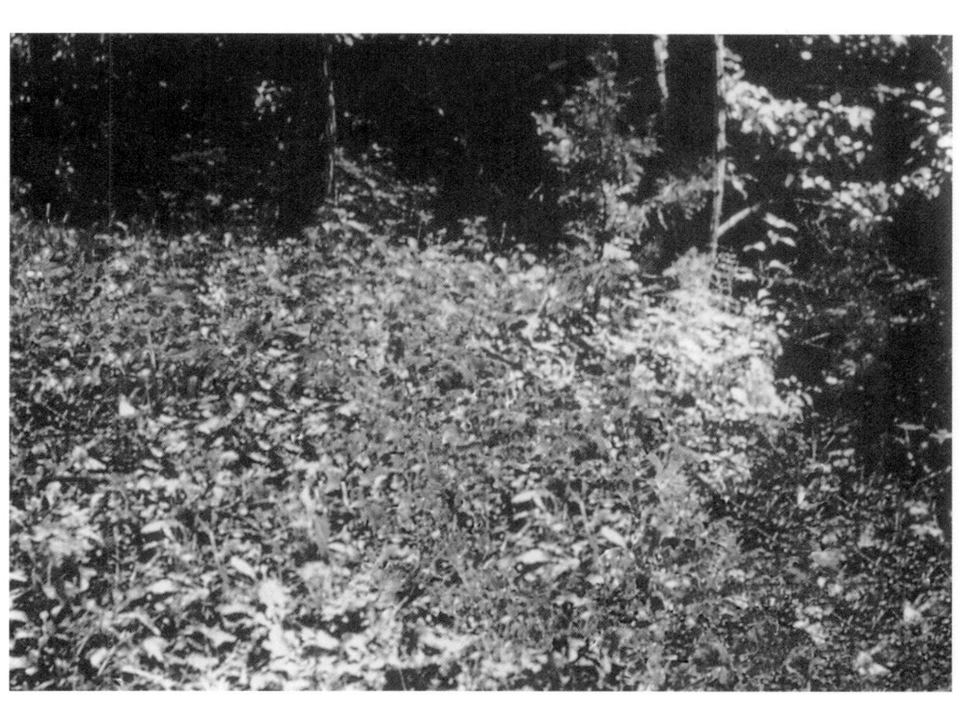

Massacre Creek Lake, Vya, Nevada, USA. 1968

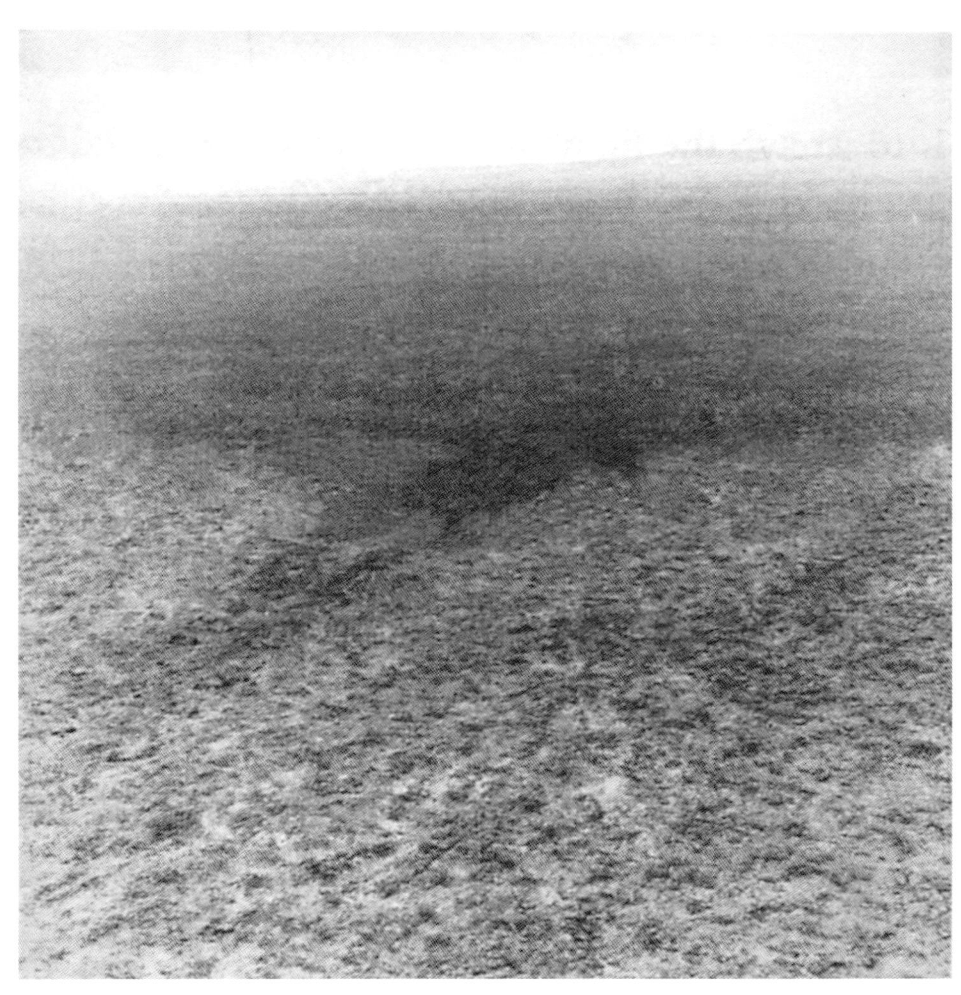

Holland. 1968

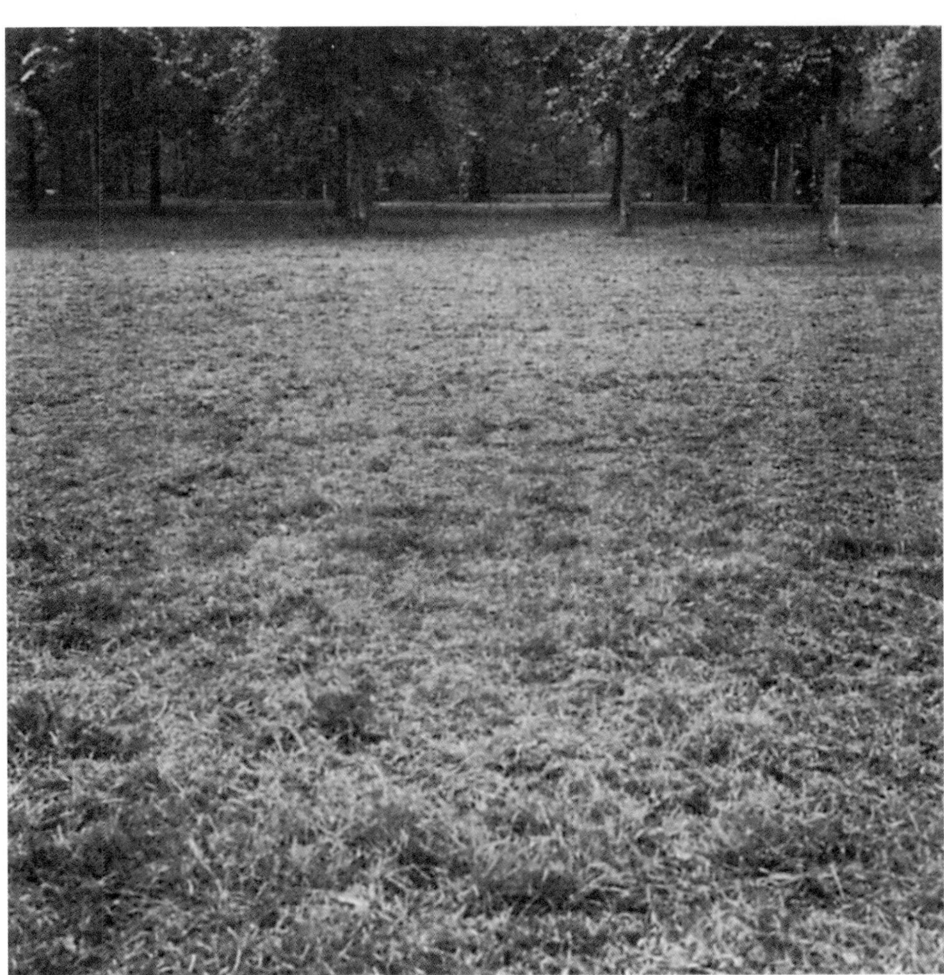

St.John River, US/Canadian Border. 1968

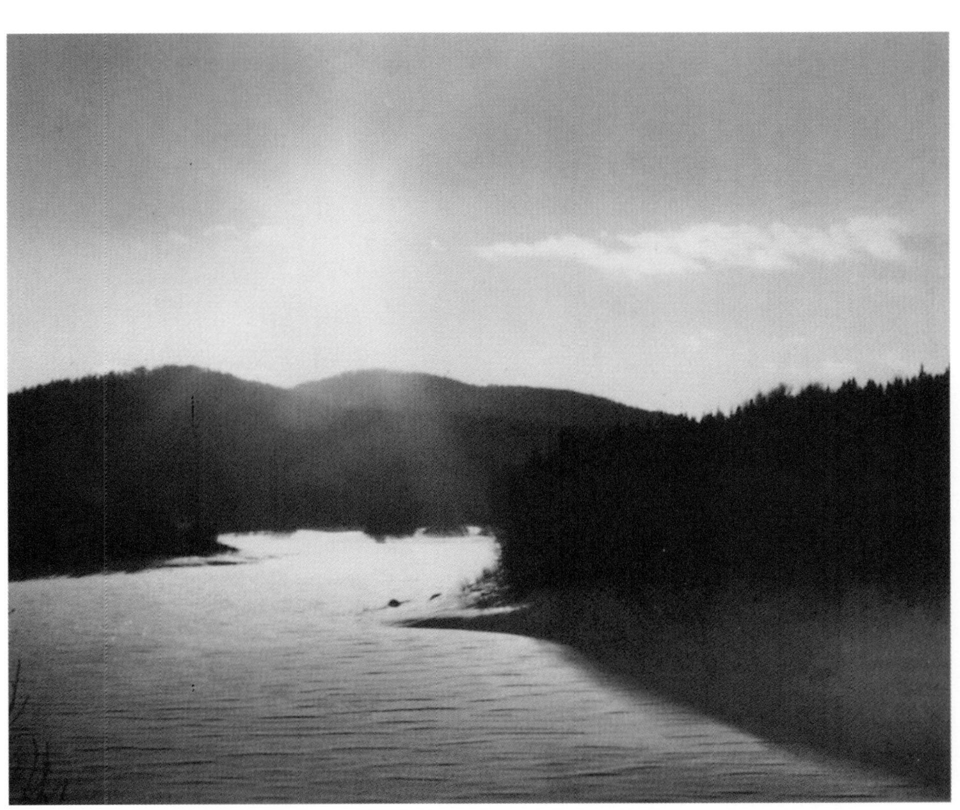

England. 1967

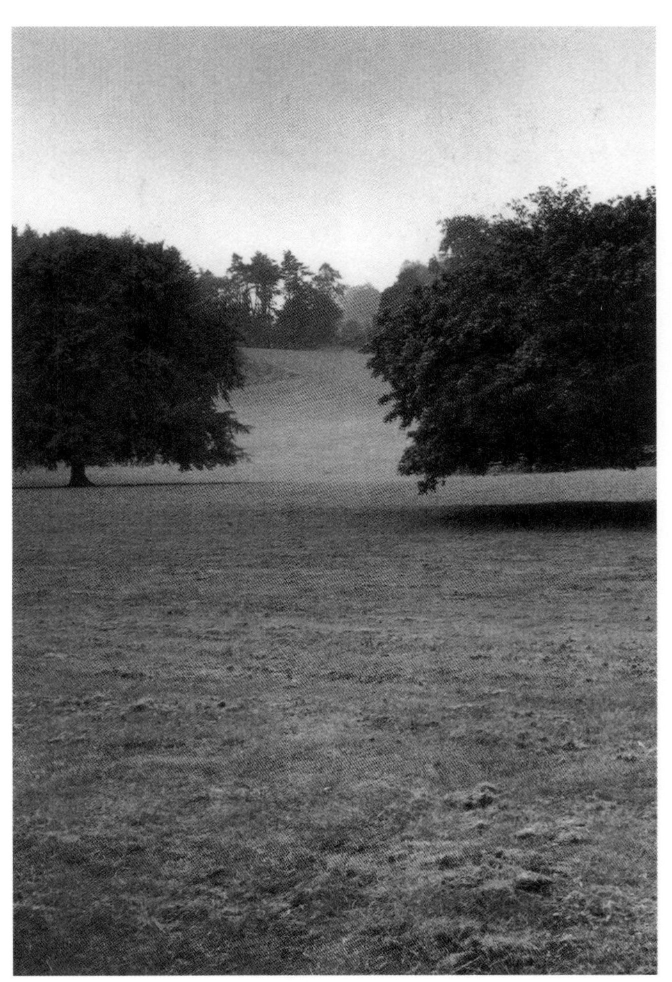

Fontenay-aux-Roses, France. October 1960

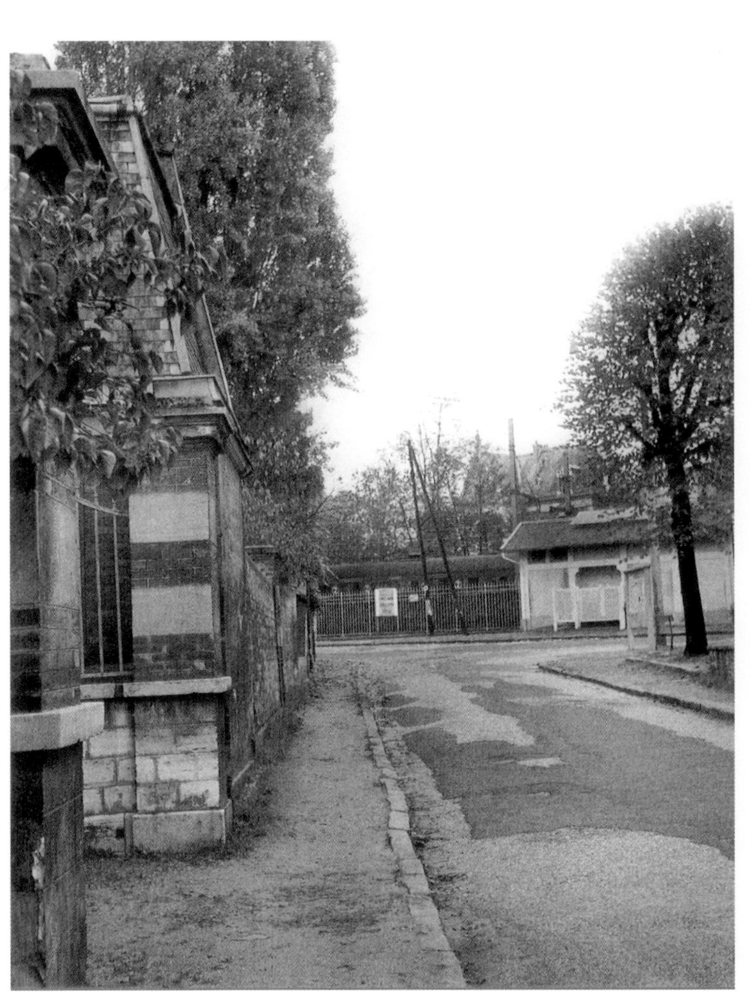